W9-ABN-276

DISCARD

DISCARD

Cougars

written and photographed by Lynn M. Stone

Lerner Publications Company • Minneapolis, Minnesota

J
599.7442
S

For Brittany, who loves cats, large and small.
                                                    —LMS

Thanks to our series consultant, Sharyn Fenwick, elementary science/math specialist. Mrs. Fenwick was the winner of the National Science Teachers Association 1991 Distinguished Teaching Award. She also was the recipient of the Presidential Award for Excellence in Math and Science Teaching, representing the state of Minnesota at the elementary level in 1992.

Early Bird Nature Books were conceptualized by Ruth Berman and designed by Steve Foley. Series editor is Joelle Goldman.

Copyright ©1997 by Lynn M. Stone
All rights reserved. International copyright secured.
No part of this book may be reproduced, stored in a retrieval system, or transmitted in any form or by any means, electronic, mechanical, photocopying, recording, or otherwise, without the prior written permission of Lerner Publications Company, except for the inclusion of brief quotations in an acknowledged review.

Library of Congress Cataloging-in-Publication Data

Stone, Lynn M.
    Cougars / written and photographed by Lynn M. Stone.
      p.   cm. — (Early bird nature books)
    Includes index.
    Summary: Describes the physical characteristics, behavior, and habitat of the members of the cat family known by several names: cougar, puma, mountain lion, and panther.
    ISBN 0-8225-3013-9 (alk. paper)
    1. Pumas—Juvenile literature. [1. Pumas.] I. Title. II. Series.
  QL737.C23S767 1997
  599.74'428—dc20   96-32696

Manufactured in the United States of America
1 2 3 4 5 6 – SP – 02 01 00 99 98 97

Contents

Map 5

Be a Word Detective 5

Chapter 1 **Cougars Are Cats** 6

Chapter 2 **Cougar Country** 10

Chapter 3 **The Hunter** 14

Chapter 4 **Cougar Talk** 26

Chapter 5 **Cougar Kittens** 30

Chapter 6 **Cougars and People** . . 38

On Sharing a Book 44
A NOTE TO ADULTS

Glossary 46

Index 47

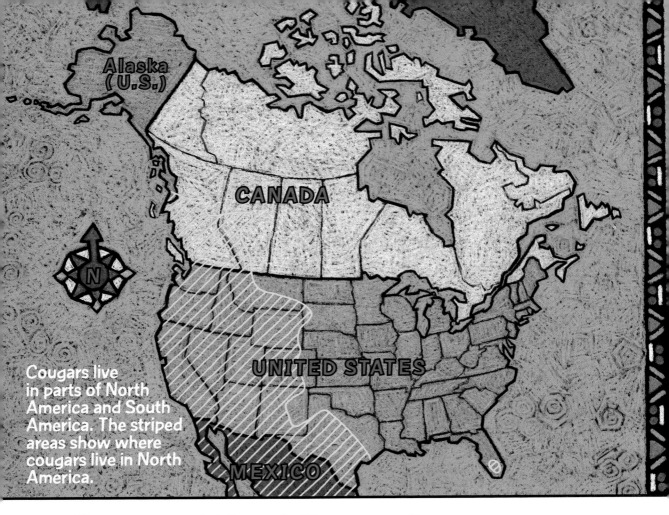

Cougars live in parts of North America and South America. The striped areas show where cougars live in North America.

Be a Word Detective

Can you find these words as you read about the cougar's life? Be a detective and try to figure out what they mean. You can turn to the glossary on page 46 for help.

carcass	kittens	prey
den	nurse	stalking
habitats	predators	territory

Chapter 1

The cougar's scientific name is Felis concolor. What are some of the cougar's nicknames?

Cougars Are Cats

You may have one nickname. But the cougar (KOO-guhr) has many. In Florida, the cougar is called the panther. People in New England call it the catamount. In other places, it's the puma, mountain lion, or painter. In Spanish, it's *el leon,* the lion.

The cougar is a cat, just as lions, tigers, jaguars, and lynxes are cats. A cougar is much like a house cat. It has the same long, smooth body. It moves like a house cat. It even sounds like a loud house cat. But a cougar is much larger than a house cat. A male cougar can weigh over 200 pounds. That's as much as 20 pet cats.

From nose to tail, a large cougar is about 8 feet long.
Its tail may be 3 feet long.

A cougar can run very fast for a short distance.

Cougars are animal athletes. Cougars
climb well. They run with great bursts of speed.
And a cougar can leap 16 feet from the ground

into a tree! That's higher than the rim of a basketball hoop. Cougars don't swim often. But they will, if they are being chased.

Cougars try to avoid getting wet. But sometimes they have to wade or swim to cross a stream.

Chapter 2

This cougar lives on land that is covered with long grass. What are some other kinds of land where cougars can live?

Cougar Country

Cougars can live in many different places. These places are called habitats. A cougar's habitat may be a desert, forest, or grassland. It may be a jungle, swamp, or mountain meadow. Cougars can live wherever they can find food. And a cougar can find a meal almost anywhere.

The mountains in Glacier National Park, Montana,
are a good home for cougars.

Many cougars live in the western United States and Canada. And some live in Florida's swamps. Cougars live in Central and South America, too.

This cougar lives in Florida. The weather in Florida is warm for most of the year.

Some places where cougars live have very cold winters. Cougars who live in cold places grow long, thick fur.

Cougars who live in cold areas are usually bigger than cougars from warmer areas. Cold country cougars also have thicker fur. Thick fur helps to keep them warm.

Chapter 3

Cougars hunt other animals for food. What kind of animal do cougars hunt the most?

The Hunter

Cougars eat meat. They are predators (PREH-duh-turz), animals who kill other animals for food. The cougar is one of the biggest predators in North and South America. Only jaguars and bears are bigger.

The animals that predators hunt are called prey. Deer are a cougar's favorite prey. Deer live in most cougar habitats. They are large animals. When a cougar kills a large animal, it has enough food to last for several days.

Jaguars live in Mexico and South America. They are larger than cougars. Jaguars are up to 9 feet long and weigh as much as 350 pounds.

Cougars are fast and strong. They are skillful hunters. They can kill big, healthy deer. But attacking a big male deer is dangerous.

The elk is a kind of deer that lives in the western United States and Canada. A male elk's antlers may be 5 feet across.

An adult elk is much bigger than a cougar. So cougars often hunt young elks, like this one.

Male deer have sharp antlers. The antlers can hurt a cougar badly. So cougars often hunt young or sick deer.

Sometimes cougars hunt smaller animals. This cougar has caught a snowshoe hare.

Sometimes a hungry cougar can't find large prey. But cougars aren't fussy. If they can't find big animals, cougars think small.

18

They will eat squirrels, raccoons, chipmunks, coyotes, foxes, rabbits, and marmots. They will even eat grasshoppers. Like house cats, cougars will eat rats and mice. Florida's cougars eat opossums and wild pigs.

This marmot could make a good meal for a cougar.

A porcupine's white quills show through its long hair.

Cougars often eat porcupines, too. But hunting these plump pincushions is tricky. The porcupine's back and tail are covered with quills. The quills are like sharp needles. The porcupine tries to swat the cougar with its prickly tail. If the porcupine hits the cougar, quills stick in the cat's face or paws. But the cougar is quick. It slides its paw under the porcupine. It flips the porcupine onto its back. Then the cougar attacks the porcupine's belly. The porcupine's belly has no sharp quills.

A cougar's prey doesn't want to be eaten. If it notices a predator, it tries to get away. So a cougar has to hunt quietly and carefully.

Deer watch and listen for danger. A cougar must be very quiet to sneak up on a deer.

The way a cougar hunts is called stalking (STAW-king). The cougar sees a deer. It creeps slowly and quietly toward the deer. The cougar stays close to the ground. It hides behind rocks, trees, and bushes. If the cougar springs forward too soon, the deer will bound away. So the cougar creeps very close to the deer. Then it attacks. It may jump onto the deer's back.

Cougars stay close to the ground as they sneak up on their prey.

A cougar is about to leap from hiding and attack its prey.

A cougar has sharp claws and teeth. It uses its claws to grab the deer. Then the cougar bites the deer's neck. The bite kills the deer. The body of the dead deer is called a carcass.

This cougar has caught a deer. The cat uses its side teeth to take bites of meat.

The cougar drags the carcass to a safe place. Then the cougar eats until it's full. It covers the rest of the carcass with leaves and twigs. Later, the cat comes back to the hiding place. It eats more meat from the carcass. When there is no meat left, the cougar must hunt again.

Cougars have rough tongues. A cougar uses its tongue to lick scraps of meat from bones.

Chapter 4

Cougars usually live alone. How do they tell other cougars to stay away?

Cougar Talk

 Cougars usually stay away from each other. Each cougar lives in an area called a territory. Each territory is one cougar's own neighborhood. It is the cat's private hunting area.

A cougar marks its territory to tell other cougars to stay away. The cougar walks along the edges of its territory. It urinates on trees and bushes. It makes little piles of droppings. The urine and droppings are territory marks. Each mark is like a No Trespassing sign. When one cougar smells another cougar's mark, it usually leaves the area.

A cougar travels long distances through its territory as it looks for food. A cougar may walk 30 miles each day.

This cougar's ears and whiskers are turned forward because it is interested in something it sees.

Cougars also say things to one another when they meet. They talk with body movements and sounds. When a cougar is angry, it lays its ears back. When it is content, it purrs. A cougar can meow, hiss, and growl.

It may make whistling noises to greet another cougar. Most of a cougar's sounds are much like a house cat's sounds. But a cougar can purr much louder!

Cougars can make loud sounds, but they can't roar. Jaguars, leopards, lions, snow leopards, and tigers are the only cats who can roar.

Chapter 5

This mother cougar is licking her kitten to clean its fur. How many kittens does a mother cougar usually have at a time?

Cougar Kittens

A female cougar may have six babies at a time. But usually she has only two or three. The baby cougars are called kittens.

Cougar kittens are born in a den. The den may be a cave. Or it may be a hollow place under a tree.

Newborn kittens are blind and helpless. Their furry coats are spotted, like a young deer's. In about two weeks, the kittens' eyes open. They take their first look at the world.

A mother cougar leaves her kittens in the den while she hunts for food.

Young kittens nurse, or drink their mother's milk. When they are six weeks old, the mother cat starts bringing meat for them to eat. The kittens grow quickly. Like house cat kittens, baby cougars are playful. They wrestle with each other and crawl about.

Even very young cougar kittens have sharp claws.

*This kitten is drinking its mother's milk. Baby cougars
drink milk until they are about three months old.*

The kittens leave the den with their mother
when they are 2 months old. For the next 18
months, the mother and her kittens travel
together.

Young kittens wait quietly while their mother hunts.
Spotted fur helps this kitten hide in the shadows.

The mother watches out for animals who might hurt her kittens. Sometimes adult male cougars kill cougar kittens. So the mother keeps her kittens away from other cougars. When the mother cat needs to go hunting, she hides her kittens in a safe place.

Cougar kittens must learn how to hunt. They practice hunting when they play. The kittens have play fights. They pounce on butterflies and chase birds.

A cougar kitten's dark spots fade as it grows up.

The mother cougar begins to take her kittens on hunting trips when they are about four months old. She takes one kitten with her at a time. The young cat follows its mother. It learns when to crouch and when to stalk. It learns when to stay still, like a cat statue. And it learns when to charge from hiding and attack its prey.

This young cougar is almost as big as its mother. Soon it will be able to take care of itself.

When the young cougars are about two years old, they are quite grown up. Each kitten has learned to hunt on its own. The mother cougar is ready to begin another family.

The kittens leave their mother. The young cougars travel together for a while. But soon they split up. Each young cat must find a territory of its own.

Chapter 6

Once cougars lived in most of the eastern United States. People killed many of these cougars. Why did people hunt cougars?

Cougars and People

Cougars once lived in most of North and South America. About 350 years ago, many people started moving to America. These people were called pioneers. The pioneers built towns and farms. They destroyed the cougars' hunting grounds.

The pioneers were hunters. They killed deer, just as the cougars did. The pioneers wanted the deer for themselves. They didn't want to share with cougars. They thought cougars were dangerous pests. The pioneers killed any cougars they found.

Some people have been killed by cougars. But most cougars stay away from people.

Later, cougars learned that sheep and cattle were good to eat. So farmers and ranchers hunted cougars, too. Cougars in the East nearly died out. In the West, the cats moved up into the mountains.

Florida is the only eastern state that still has wild cougars. In 1996, about 40 cougars lived in the Big Cypress Swamp in Florida.

Vancouver Island, in Canada, is home to many cougars. Many others live just outside the city of Vancouver.

Cougars usually avoid people. But more and more people live and travel in cougar habitats. People are changing more wild land into farms and towns. There are fewer prey animals for cougars to hunt. So cougars have to travel farther to find food. Sometimes they look for food where people live.

Cars have hit and killed many cougars in Florida. This sign warns drivers to watch out for cougars.

In some places, people still hunt cougars. The hunters use dogs to find the cats. The dogs have keen noses. They can smell a cougar. The dogs follow the cougar's smell. The cougar runs from the barking dogs. As the dogs come near, the frightened cougar climbs a tree. The dogs stay under the tree. They watch the cat until the hunters come. Then the hunters can shoot the cougar.

42

But in many places laws protect cougars. The western United States and Canada have huge parks. Many of these parks are safe homes for cougars. In the parks, cougars can lead their secret, shadowy lives.

People are helping wild cougars to stay alive.

On Sharing a Book

As you know, adults greatly influence a child's attitude toward reading. When a child sees you read, or when you share a book with a child, you're sending a message that reading is important. Show the child that reading a book together is important to you. Find a comfortable, quiet place. Turn off the television and limit other distractions like telephone calls.

Be prepared to start slowly. Take turns reading parts of this book. Stop and talk about what you're reading. Talk about the photographs. You may find that much of the shared time is spent discussing just a few pages. This discussion time is valuable for both of you, so don't move through the book too quickly. If the child begins to lose interest, stop reading. Continue sharing the book at another time. When you do pick up the book again, be sure to revisit the parts you have already read. Most importantly, enjoy the book!

Be a Vocabulary Detective

You will find a word list on page 5. Words selected for this list are important to the understanding of the topic of this book. Encourage the child to be a word detective and search for the words as you read the book together. Talk about what the words mean and how they are used in the sentence. Do any of these words have more than one meaning? You will find these words defined in a glossary on page 46.

What about Questions?

Use questions to make sure the child understands the information in this book. Here are some suggestions:

> What did this paragraph tell us? What does this picture show? What do you think we'll learn about next? Other than cougars, how many kinds of cats can you name? Could a cougar live in your backyard? Why/Why not? How do cougars mark their territories? How do cougars get their food? How is a cougar family like your family, and how is it different? What do you think it's like being a cougar? What is your favorite part of the book? Why?

If the child has questions, don't hesitate to respond with questions of your own like: What do *you* think? Why? What is it that you don't know? If the child can't remember certain facts, turn to the index.

Introducing the Index

The index is an important learning tool. It helps readers get information quickly without searching throughout the whole book. Turn to the index on page 47. Choose an entry, such as *claws,* and ask the child to use the index to find out how cougars use their claws. Repeat this exercise with as many entries as you like. Ask the child to point out the differences between an index and a glossary. (The index helps readers find information quickly, while the glossary tells readers what words mean.)

Where in the World?

Many plants and animals found in the Early Bird Nature Books series live in parts of the world other than the United States. Encourage the child to find the places mentioned in this book on a world map or globe. Take time to talk about climate, terrain, and how you might live in such places.

All the World in Metric!

Although our monetary system is in metric units (based on multiples of 10), the United States is one of the few countries in the world that does not use the metric system of measurement. Here are some conversion activities you and the child can do using a calculator:

WHEN YOU KNOW:	MULTIPLY BY:	TO FIND:
miles	1.602	kilometers
feet	0.3048	meters
inches	2.54	centimeters
gallons	3.787	liters
tons	0.907	metric tons
pounds	0.454	kilograms

Activities

Make up a story about cougars. Be sure to include information from this book. Draw or paint pictures to illustrate your story.

Pretend you're a cougar. Have a friend pretend to be a deer who is eating grass. Quietly sneak up on your friend. Stay low to the ground and hide behind furniture or bushes. How close can you get before your friend notices you? Next, pretend to be the deer and have your friend stalk you.

Glossary

carcass—the body of a dead animal

den—a hidden, safe place. Baby cougars live in a den until they are about two months old.

habitats—areas where a kind of animal can live and grow

kittens—baby cougars

nurse—to drink mother's milk

predators (PREH-duh-turz)—animals who hunt other animals for food

prey—animals who are hunted and eaten by other animals

stalking (STAW-king)—hunting an animal by sneaking up on it

territory—an animal's very own place. A cougar marks its territory so other cougars will stay away.

Index

Pages listed in **bold** type refer to photographs.

claws, 23, **32**

dangers, 16-17, 34, 42

eating, 14-15, 24-25, 32, **33**

fur, 13, 31, **34, 35**

growing up, **35,** 37

homes, 26-27, 37
hunting, 14-25, **27,** 35-37, 41

jumping, 8-9

kittens, 30-37

location, 10-13, 38, 40, **41,** 43

names, 6

people and cougars, 38-43
playing, 32, 35

size, 7
sounds, 7, 28-29
speed, 8

tail, **7**
teeth, 23, **24**
tongue, **25, 30**

About the Author

Lynn M. Stone is an author and photographer who has written more than 250 books for young readers about wildlife and natural history, including Lerner's Early Bird Nature Books titles *Penguins* and *Swans.* In addition to photographing wildlife, Mr. Stone enjoys fishing and traveling. A former teacher, he lives with his wife and daughter in Batavia, Illinois.

J
599.7442
S

Stone, Lynn M.
   Cougars.

DISCARD

Hiram Halle Memorial Library
Pound Ridge, New York